Creative Beaded Jewelry

Sigal Buzaglo

sixth&spring
books
New York, NY

sixth&spring
books

Produced for SOHO Publishing Company by Penn Publishing Ltd.
www.penn.co.il
Editor: Shoshana Brickman
Design and layout: Michal & Dekel
Photography: Roee Feinburg
Styling: Roni Chen
Makeup artist: Perry Halfon

Library of Congress Cataloging-in-Publication Data

Buzaglo, Sigal.
  Creative Beaded Jewelry / By Sigal Buzaglo. -- First Edition.
    pages cm
  ISBN 978-1-936096-10-7
  1. Beadwork. 2. Jewelry making. I. Title.
  TT860.B89 2011
  745.58'2--dc22
                    2010041711

ISBN-13: 978-1-936096-10-7
Manufactured in China
3 5 7 9 10 8 6 4
First Edition

 # Contents

 # *Introduction*

There is no limit to the range of jewelry that can be made with beautiful beads. You can make a pair of delicate dangly earrings, an elegant shimmering necklace, or a surprisingly simple crystal bracelet. All you need are clear instructions, a few tools and materials, and you're ready to go. In no time at all, you'll be wearing brilliantly beaded jewelry that you made yourself!

Creative Beaded Jewelry contains dozens of stylish jewelry projects to suit every taste and skill level. Every project comes with specific instructions and lots of color photographs to demonstrate exactly how certain stages should look. Projects are ranked according to skill levels, but don't let this deter you from selecting something that is above (or below) your own level of experience. All of the projects are bright, rewarding and fun to make.

Many of the projects combine materials you may never have thought to combine or use materials in unusual ways. For example, the **Striking Silver and Leather Necklace** (pages 72 to 75) uses jump rings as part of the decorative element and not just to connect components. In the **Leather Cornucopia Necklace** (pages 52 to 55), pearls, crystals and leather cord are combined in a uniquely elegant manner.

While every project comes with a precise description of the materials, feel free to replace colors and components as you like. In this way, you can create beaded jewelry that is distinctly your own.

About the Author

Sigal Buzaglo has operated a successful beaded jewelry shop in Tel Aviv's chic Neve Tzedek neighborhood for more than a decade. She was drawn to the field of jewelry-making out of a love of creating things with her own two hands and a never-ending supply of ideas.

Sigal has attended and participated in exhibitions across Europe, and constantly incorporates new materials and techniques into her jewelry. Sigal loves to travel and often seeks out new ideas while abroad. Many of her projects are inspired by the color combinations and styles she sees while exploring different countries and cultures.

Using this Book

The projects in this book are ranked according to skill level. Use these levels to guide you in your project selection, but don't let them stop you from trying something out of your range.

Easy If this is your first time making beaded jewelry, these projects are right for you.

Intermediate These projects are perfect for readers with a bit of beading experience.

Advanced These projects call for a variety of techniques.

Challenging These projects are call for a variety of techniques and materials. They may require careful planning.

MATERIALS

Beads

You'll find a limitless selection of beads these days, in every size, shape, color and price range. When making the projects in this book, you may choose to use the same beads as photographed, or replace them with something similar (or different!). Here are descriptions of some of my favorite types of beads.

Crystal beads

These sparkling beads add dazzle to any beaded project. They come in a variety of shapes, sizes and finishes. Swarovski and Czech crystals are known for their high quality.

Gemstone beads

Gemstones add a natural look and feel to beaded jewelry. They come in various shapes, sizes and textures.

Lampwork beads

These vibrant beads were traditionally handmade using torches and colored glass. Using just a few of these in a project adds immense color and beauty.

Metal beads

These come in silver, gold and pewter, and a vast array of shapes and sizes. Metallic rondelle beads look like flattened disks and are often inserted between round beads to add a decorative touch.

Millefiori beads

Also known as mosaic beads, these glass beads feature tiny designs and come in diverse shapes and colors.

Pearls

Classic and smooth, pearls naturally add elegance to any design. They may be perfectly round or have a textured surface. Though most pearls are lustrous white, they come in other colors as well.

Seed beads

These tiny beads come in a variety of colors and finishes. They are measured according to size rather than length; the larger the size, the smaller the bead. In other words, 11° beads are smaller than 6°. Ordinary seed beads are rounded; 2-cut seed beads have flat sides. Seed beads are generally sold by weight; this is how they are measured in the projects in this book.

Stringing materials

A variety of materials may be used to string beads. These materials can be found at bead stores, hobby stores or online.

Stringing materials, in clockwise direction from top: cotton cord, wire, nylon-coated stainless steel beading wire, link chain, organza ribbon, nylon beading thread, elastic beading cord.

Chains

In addition to using chains to string pendants, decorated eye pins and head pins can be strung onto individual chain links. Chains can also be cut into pieces and connected to beads and other findings.

Cotton cord

This comes in a variety of colors and is ideal for making jewelry in which the stringing material is visible. Make sure you select beads with holes that are large enough to slide onto the cord you choose.

Elastic beading cord

This flexible cord is often used to make bracelets. Using this cord means you won't need to use a clasp to secure the bracelet.

Leather cord

Using leather cord for beaded jewelry often creates a lovely effect; the smoothness of the beads contrasts with the texture of the leather cord. When using leather cord, make sure that the cord tips and crimp beads you use have a large enough hole. Bolo cord is braided leather cord that comes in various widths and colors.

Memory wire

This coiled wire is rigid and keeps its form. It comes in various sizes, suitable for making necklaces, bracelets, anklets and rings. Jewelry made with memory wire does not require a clasp.

Nylon beading thread

This transparent thread is commonly used for beaded projects.

Nylon-coated stainless steel beading wire

This is a popular type of stringing material that is both durable and flexible. It comes in various widths.

Organza ribbon

This delicate fabric can be used to make lovely beaded jewelry. I recommend singeing the ends so that they don't fray. Wrap the singed end with sewing thread for easy stringing.

Wire

A wide variety of wires can be used to make beaded jewelry. Be sure you select wire that won't rust or corrode, since you want your jewelry to last. Check the gauge of the wire you select and make sure the holes in your beads fit comfortably on the wire.

Findings

These small metal components are used to connect, secure, hang and close beaded jewelry. They come in diverse materials and are sold at a wide range of prices. To ensure that your jewelry lasts a long time, select high quality findings.

Bead caps

Use these to dress up ordinary beads by stringing them on one or both sides of the bead. They come in various sizes, designs and colors. Make sure that the bead cap suits the size of the bead it will accompany.

Crimp beads

These are used to secure the ends of beading wire or cord. They can also be used to secure the position of beads on beading wire. They come in various sizes, so make sure you select crimp beads that are right for your stringing material.

Charms

Made from metal, stone or glass, these dangling findings add a decorative touch. I often use leaf and heart charms but there are dozens of designs to choose from.

Ear wires and hoop earrings

These are used to make earrings. They come in various shapes, sizes and styles.

Clasps

These are used to secure necklaces and bracelets. Lobster claw clasps are the most common type but you may prefer decorative clasps such as toggle clasps or hook-and-eye clasps.

Connector bars

These are used to connect parts of jewelry to each other or to the clasp. They often come with several loops.

Cord tips

Also known as cord ends or crimp ends, these are used to connect stringing materials to clasps. The projects in this book use bend-style cord tips, but you may use ones that are crimped or glued.

Head pins and eye pins

These are used to string beads and connect them. They are made from diverse metals, and come in various gauges and lengths. Head pins have a flat bottom; eye pins have a loop at the bottom.

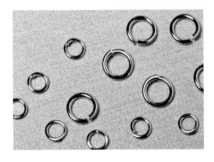

Jump rings

These small rings are used to connect elements. They are made from various materials and come in different widths and sizes. All of the jump rings used in this book are unsoldered. This means they can be opened and closed using two pliers.

Spacer bars

These are used to separate beads in a design. They often come with several loops.

TOOLS

You don't need a drawer full of tools to make beautiful beaded jewelry. In fact, all of the projects in this book were made using just a few simple tools. I recommend buying high-quality tools that are comfortable to use and will last a long time.

Flat-nose pliers
These are used to flatten crimp beads and crimp ends. You can also use them to grasp one side of a jump ring when opening and closing it.

Round-nose pliers
These are used to make loops in eye pins and head pins. You can also use them to grasp one side of a jump ring when opening and closing it.

Pliers
You'll find a wide variety of pliers used in beaded jewelry-making. Some pliers are made for one specific purpose. Other pliers can be used for multiple purposes. All the projects in this book can be made using two basic types of pliers:

Scissors
Use sharp sturdy scissors to cut beading wire, leather cord and cotton cord.

Wire cutters
These are used to cut beading wire and to trim head pins and eye pins.

BASIC TECHNIQUES

Every single project in this book is distinct, but all of them are made using just a few basic techniques. Once you learn these, you'll be able to make all of these projects, along with countless others.

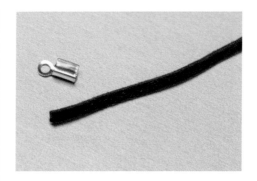 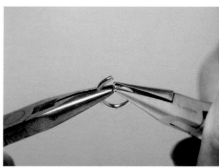

Securing ends with crimp beads

Crimp beads can be used to secure the ends of necklaces and bracelets. I generally use tw
crimp beads on each end, to ensure a secure finish.

1. String two crimp beads onto the beading wire.
2. Make a loop at the end of the wire and insert the tip of the wire back into the crimp beads.
3. Flatten the crimp beads with flat-nose pliers and trim the excess wire with wire cutters.

Securing ends with cord tips

Cord tips are strung onto the ends of chains or cords. All of the projects in this book use bend-style cord tips.

1. Insert the chain or cord end into the cord tip.
2. Fold over the sides of the cord tip using flat-nose pliers.

 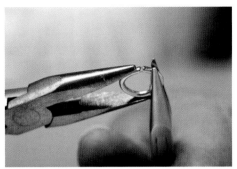  

Opening and closing jump rings

You'll need two sets of pliers to open jump rings and almost any type will do. I generally use one pair of flat-nose pliers and one pair of round-nose pliers, but you can use other types of pliers if you like. Jump rings are never opened by drawing the ends sideways away from each other. They are always opened by drawing one end forwards and the other end backwards.

Making a loop in a head pin or eye pin

These dull-tipped pins are often used to hang one or several beads. When selecting the head pins or eye pins for your project, make sure the gauge of the pin is right for your beads.

To open

1. Hold a set of pliers in each hand. Hold the jump ring so that the O is visible to you and grasp each side of the jump ring with a set of pliers.

2. Move one set of pliers away from you and the other set of pliers towards you.

3. Continue moving the pliers in opposite directions until the open space in the jump ring is large enough for stringing.

To close

1. Hold a set of pliers in each hand. Grasp each side of the open jump ring with one set of pliers.

2. Move the pliers that are farther from you towards you. Move the pliers that are closer to you away from you.

3. Continue moving the pliers until the two ends of the jump ring meet.

1. String the bead or beads onto the head pin or eye pin.

2. Trim the wire to ⅜" (1 cm) and bend the head pin at a 90° using flat-nose pliers.

3. Grasp the tip of the wire with round-nose pliers and shape into a loop.

Precociously Pink Bracelet

The beauty in this piece lies in its sparkling crystals and delicate seed beads.
If you make this design for a friend, adding an extension chain
means the bracelet will be adjustable.

FINISHED MEASUREMENT	TOOLS	SKILL LEVEL
6" (15 cm)	*Scissors* *Flat-nose pliers* *Round-nose pliers*	

MATERIALS

*30" (75 cm) nylon-coated stainless steel beading
wire, 0.022" (0.55 mm)*

20 antique gold-plated crimp beads, 1.5 mm

2 gold-plated 4-loop connector bars

66 pink round faceted crystal beads, 5 mm

6 decorated antique gold beads, 4 mm

2 antique gold-plated 5-loop spacer bars

8 gold-plated rondelle beads, 4 mm

5 grams brown seed beads, 11°

10 grams transparent gold seed beads, 6°

2 gold-plated jump rings, 5 mm

1 antique gold-plated lobster claw clasp

Extension chain

2" (5 cm) gold-plated, small-link chain

1 gold-plated head pin, 2 cm

1 crystal bead, 4 mm

(continued on page 18)

(continued from page 16)

1. Strand 1: Cut a 6" (15 cm) piece of beading wire. String 2 crimp beads onto the beading wire and draw the wire through the first loop in one connector bar. Tuck the tip of the beading wire back into the crimp beads and flatten the crimp beads.

2. String 3 crystal beads, 1 decorated gold bead, 3 crystal beads and 1 decorated gold bead onto the beading wire. String the wire through the first loop in one spacer bar. String 3 crystal beads, 1 decorated gold bead, 3 crystal beads, 1 decorated gold bead and 3 crystal beads onto the beading wire. String the wire through the first loop in the other spacer bar.

3. String 3 crystal beads, 1 decorated gold bead and 3 crystal beads onto the beading wire. String 2 crimp beads onto this end of the beading wire and string the wire through the first loop in the other connector bar.

4. Tuck the tip of the beading wire back into the crimp beads and flatten the crimp beads.

5. Strand 2: Repeat step 1 but attach this piece of beading wire to the second loop in one connector bar. String 7 crystal beads onto the beading wire, then string the wire through the second hole in the first spacer bar. String 11 crystal beads onto the beading wire; then string the wire through the second loop in the other spacer bar. String on 7 crystal beads, then 2 crimp beads. String the wire through the second loop in the other connector bar and repeat step 4 to secure the beading wire.

6. Strand 3: Repeat step 1 but attach this piece of beading wire to the third loop in one connector bar, then string on the beads in the following order:
2 crystal beads, 1 gold rondelle bead, 2 crystal beads, 1 gold rondelle bead and 2 crystal beads.

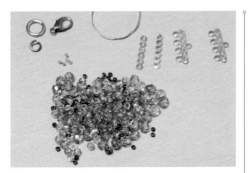

Materials

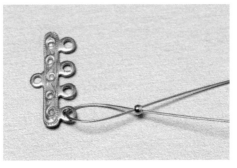

String on a crimp bead and flatten to secure

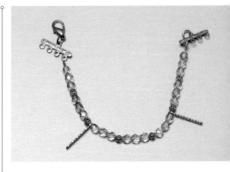

Measure the strand, then attach the secon connector bar

7. String the wire through the third hole in the spacer bar, then repeat the pattern in step 6 to string 10 crystal beads and 4 gold rondelle beads onto the beading wire. Connect the wire to the third loop of the other connector bar.

8. Strand 4: Repeat step 1 but attach this piece of beading wire to the fourth loop in one connector bar, then string on brown seed beads until you reach the first spacer bar. Draw the beading wire through the fourth loop in the spacer bar, then string on brown seed beads until you reach the next spacer bar. Draw the beading wire through the fourth loop in this spacer bar, then string on seed beads until the strand is the right length. String on 2 crimp beads and secure the beading wire to the fourth loop in the connector bar.

9. Strand 5: Attach the fifth piece of beading wire to the fourth loop in the connector bar, then string on gold seed beads until you reach the first spacer bar. Draw the wire through the fifth loop in the spacer bar, then string on gold seed beads until you reach the next spacer bar. Draw the beading wire through the fifth loop in this spacer bar, then string on seed beads until the strand is the right length. String on 2 crimp beads; then secure the beading wire to the fourth loop in the connector bar.

10. Open both jump rings and string one through each connector bar. Attach the clasp to one jump ring and close the jump ring.

11. Extension chain: String one end of the 2" (5 cm) chain onto the other jump ring and close the jump ring. String the 4 mm crystal bead onto the 2 cm head pin and trim the ead pin to ⅜" (1 cm). Make a loop in the head pin, draw it through the last link in the chain and close the loop.

Secure each end of each strand with two crimp beads

Add an extension chain for flexible sizing

Bountiful Vineyard Bracelet

This indulgent bracelet features several strands of richly colored beads held together by a string of beads. The combination of purple and gold colors is evocative of a vineyard at harvest time.

FINISHED MEASUREMENT	TOOLS	SKILL LEVEL
7.5" (19 cm)	*Scissors* *Flat-nose pliers* *Ripe-nose pliers*	●●○○

MATERIALS

98" (250 cm) transparent elastic beading cord, 0.8 mm

40 red faceted crystal beads, 5 mm

30 brown faceted beads, 7 mm

1 turquoise faceted opaque crystal bead, 9 mm

2 gold-plated bead caps

40 pale yellow faceted crystal beads, 5 mm

30 gold round beads, 7 mm

20 grams transparent gold seed beads, 6°

10 grams matte brown seed beads, 6°

4 gold-plated charms, various shapes, 1 cm

4 gold-plated jump rings, 6 mm

3 grams transparent brown seed beads, 11°

6" (15 cm) transparent nylon beading thread

(continued on page 22)

(continued from page 20)

1. String red crystal beads onto the beading cord until about 7½" (19 cm) of cord are beaded.

2. Wrap the beaded cord around your wrist to make sure the size is right. Add or subtract beads as necessary, then cut the cord and tie the ends together in a knot to form a bracelet.

3. Repeat steps 1 and 2 to make a bracelet of brown crystal beads. Integrate 1 turquoise bead sandwiched by 2 gold-plated bead caps onto this bracelet.

4. Repeat steps 1 and 2 to make 1 bracelet of pale yellow crystal beads, 2 bracelets of gold seed beads, 1 bracelet of brown seed beads and 1 bracelet of gold round beads. Open the jump rings and use them to string a charm onto each bracelet if you like.

5. String the brown seed beads onto the beading thread until the beaded length is about 4¾" (12 cm). Hold all 7 beaded bracelets together and wrap the strand from step 5 twice around the bracelets to secure them in a bunch. Tie the ends of the strand together in a secure knot.

Materials

String on beads until beaded cord is the right length

I recommend working straight from the spool of elastic beading cord when you make this bracelet. I find this method is more convenient and cuts down on wasted beading cord.

Use jump rings to affix charms

Wrap the strand of brown seed beads twice around all 7 beaded bracelets

Royal Harvest Bracelet

Rich in red and golden round beads, this bracelet
is a brilliant accessory for day or night. It looks lovely when worn
with the Luscious Cherry Earrings (pages 140 to 143).

FINISHED MEASUREMENT	TOOLS	SKILL LEVEL

FINISHED MEASUREMENT

7" (18 cm)

TOOLS

Wire cutters
Round-nose pliers
Flat-nose pliers

MATERIALS

30 red and gold beads, various shapes, 2 to 4 mm
10 red and gold beads, various shapes, 8 mm
10 red and gold beads, various shapes, 6 mm
6 red and gold beads, various shapes, 10 mm
20 gold-plated bead caps
62 gold-plated head pins, 2 cm
7" (18 cm) gold-plated, small-link chain
2 gold plated jump rings, 5 mm
1 gold-plated clasp
Extension chain
2" (5 cm) gold-plated, small-link chain
1 gold-plated head pin, 2 cm
1 crystal bead, 4 mm

(continued on page 26)

(continued from page 24)

1. Arrange the beads on your work surface in the order you want for the bracelet. Place smaller beads at both ends and larger beads in the middle.

2. When you are satisfied with the arrangement, string each bead onto a head pin. String a bead cap onto some of the head pins before stringing the bead. Trim each head pin to ⅜" (1 cm) and make a loop. Don't close the loop.

3. Starting at one end of the 7" (18 cm) chain, string a small bead onto each link for about 1¼" (3 cm) of the chain.

4. Repeat step 3 at the other end of the chain.

5. Continue by stringing an 8 mm bead onto each link in the chain for ¾" (2 cm) on both sides of end of the chain.

6. Fill the 3¼" (8 cm) in the middle of the chain by attaching the 10 mm beads at even intervals. Attach the rest of the 8 mm beads to this part of the chain at regular intervals.

7. Open both jump rings. String one jump ring through the last link on each end of the chain. String the clasp onto one jump ring and close the jump ring.

8. Extension chain: String one end of the 2" (5 cm) chain onto the other jump ring and close the jump ring. String the 4 mm crystal bead onto the 2 cm head pin and trim the head pin to ⅜" (1 cm). Make a loop in the head pin, draw it through the last link in the chain and close the loop.

Materials

String a looped head pin onto a link and close the loop

Attach looped head pins all along the chai

This design is an excellent way of using leftover beads from other projects. Use beads of similar colors for a bold impact.

When making bracelets as a gift, add an extension chain so that the bracelet size is flexible.

Vintage Crystal Bracelet

This shimmering bracelet is chic, whether dressed up or down, yet very simple to make. Optimize its beauty by selecting high-quality crystals and extra-special head pins.

FINISHED MEASUREMENT	TOOLS	SKILL LEVEL
6" (15 cm)	*Wire cutters* *Round-nose pliers* *Flat-nose pliers*	

MATERIALS

120 transparent gray, faceted rondelle crystal beads, 9 mm
120 silver-plated head pins with ball, 3.5 cm
11" (26 cm) transparent elastic beading cord, 1 mm

(continued on page 30)

(continued from page 28)

1. String each bead onto a head pin. Trim each head pin to ⅜" (1 cm) and make a double loop.

2. String the head pins onto the beading cord.

3. Position the beads on either side of the cord in order to fit the maximum number of beads for a really rich look.

4. When the bracelet is the right length, tie together the ends with several secure knots.

Materials

String each bead onto a head pin

Making consistently shaped loops can be tricky, so practice with a few ordinary head pins before you start making this bracelet using ball-topped head pins.

String the decorated head pins onto the beading cord

Adjust the beads so that they fit closely together

Sterling Garden Bracelet

This delicate bracelet is just right
for dressing up a simple jean ensemble.
It's also perfect for showing off a handful of pretty beads.

FINISHED MEASUREMENT

7½" (19 cm)

TOOLS

Wire cutters
Flat-nose pliers
Round-nose pliers

SKILL LEVEL

MATERIALS

3¼" (8 cm) piece of silver-plated, non-soldered link chain, 7 mm links
4 turquoise and red lampwork beads, 15 mm
8 silver-plated square bead caps, 10 mm
4 silver-plated eye pins, 4 cm
6 silver-plated flowers, 15 mm, with 5 mm hole
6 silver-plated rectangular rings, 12 mm
1 silver-plated clasp

(continued on page 34)

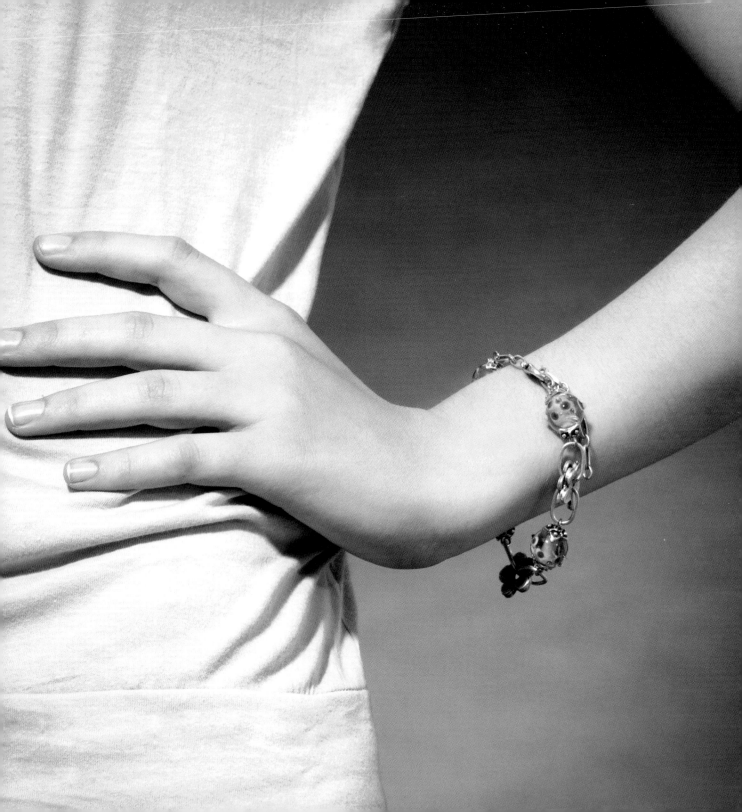

(continued from page 32)

1. Cut the chain into two pieces, one measuring 2" (5 cm) and the other measuring ¾" (2 cm).

2. Sandwich a lampwork bead between two bead caps. String the bead caps and bead onto an eye pin and trim the eye pin to ⅜" (1 cm). Make a closed loop.

3. Repeat step 2 to string the other beads and bead caps onto eye pins.

4. Open two rectangular jump rings. String one jump ring through the loops on either end of a bead. String 2 silver-plated flowers onto each jump ring and close the jump rings.

5. Open two rectangular jump rings and string one through each pair of flowers that were strung in step 4.

6. Attach one bead to each of the open jump rings and close the jump rings.

7. Repeat step 4 to attach one more pair of flowers to the bracelet. Open one rectangular jump ring to attach the remaining bead to this pair of flowers and close the jump ring.

8. Attach the 2" (5 cm) piece of chain to one end of the bracelet and the ¾" (2 cm) piece of chain to the other.

9. Open the last link on the ¾" (2 cm) chain and string on the clasp. Close the link.

Materials

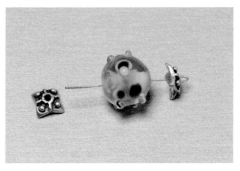

Sandwich a bead between bead caps and string onto an eye pin

Follow this basic design but alter the theme for a different look. For example, replace the silver-plated flowers with butterflies or hearts.

Connect pairs of silver-plated flowers on either side of a bead

Connect the beads and flowers in an alternating pattern

Trendy Twisted Bracelet

This wire and bead bracelet features a bright collection
of seed beads wrapped around smooth leather cord.
Funky and fun, it evokes a sense of crisp autumn weather!

FINISHED MEASUREMENT	TOOLS	SKILL LEVEL
7" (17.5 cm)	*Scissors*	
	Flat-nose pliers	
	Round-nose pliers	
	Wire cutters	

MATERIALS

24" (64 cm) leather cord, 2 mm
2 gold-plated cord tips, 2 mm
1 gold-plated lobster claw clasp
2 gold-plated jump rings, 5 mm
22" (56 cm) bronze wire, 24-gauge (0.5 mm)
20 grams seed beads assorted colors, 6°

(continued on page 38)

(continued from page 36)

1. Cut the cord into four 6" (15 cm) pieces and hold all 4 pieces together. Insert one end of all 4 cords into a cord tip and flatten the cord tip.

2. Repeat step 1 on the other side of the cords.

3. Open the jump rings and insert one jump ring into each cord tip. Attach the clasp to one of the jump rings. Close both jump rings.

4. Measure 1½" (4 cm) from one end of the cords and wrap one end of the bronze wire several times around all 4 cords until the wire is securely attached.

5. String beads onto the bronze wire until about 19" (48 cm) of wire is beaded. After all the beads have been strung, begin wrapping the beaded wire around the leather cords to form a tight coil of beaded wire.

6. Continue wrapping the beaded wire until you are about 1½" (4 cm) from the other cord tip. Wrap bare bronze wire several times around all 4 cords to secure this end of the wire. Tuck the tip of the wire under the beaded wire to hide it.

Materials

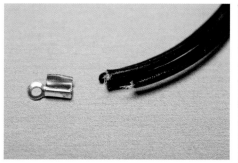

Tuck one end of all four cords into a cord tip

Attach the clasp to a cord tip using a jump ring

For a more delicate look, choose smaller seed beads. To make a bracelet to suit winter wear, choose beads that are various shades of blue and white.

String beads onto the wire in a random pattern

Wrap the beaded wire around the cords in a tight spiral

Wrap the end of the wire around the cords to secure

Hollywood Glamour Bracelet

This bracelet evokes the classic Hollywood style of the 1940s and 50s.
Fairly simple to make, there's nothing simple about its impact.

FINISHED MEASUREMENT	TOOLS	SKILL LEVEL
6½" (16.5 cm)	*Scissors*	

MATERIALS

90 opaque white multifaceted round crystal beads, 8 mm
20 opaque pink multifaceted round crystal beads, 8 mm
4 rounded rectangle silver-plated 5-strand spacer bars
60" (152 cm) transparent elastic beading cord, 0.8 mm

(continued on page 42)

(continued from page 40)

1. Strand 1: String 5 white crystal beads onto the beading cord. Draw the cord through the first hole on the first spacer bar.

2. String on 6 white crystal beads, then draw the cord through the first hole on the second spacer bar. String 5 white crystal beads onto the beading cord; then draw the cord through the first hole on the third spacer bar.

3. String on 6 white crystal beads, then draw the cord through the first hole on the fourth spacer bar. Cut the beading cord and tie the ends together in a secure triple knot.

4. Strand 2: String 2 white crystal beads, 1 pink crystal bead and 2 white crystal beads onto the beading cord. Draw the cord through the second hole on the first spacer bar.

5. String on 2 white crystal beads, 2 pink crystal beads and 2 white crystal beads; then draw the cord through the second hole on the second spacer bar.

6. Repeat steps 4 and 5, stringing the cord through the second hole in the third and fourth spacer bars. Cut the beading cord and tie both ends together in a secure knot.

7. Strand 3: String 1 white crystal bead, 1 pink crystal bead, 1 white crystal bead, 1 pink crystal bead and 1 white crystal on the beading cord. Draw the cord through the third hole on the first spacer bar.

8. String 1 white crystal bead, 1 pink crystal bead, 2 white crystal beads, 1 pink crystal bead and 1 white crystal bead onto the beading cord. Draw the cord through the third hole on the second spacer bar.

9. Repeat steps 7 and 8, stringing the cord through the third hole in the third and fourth spacer bars. Cut the

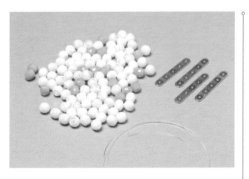

Materials

Connect the first beaded strand with a secure triple knot

For Strand 3, alternate between white and pink beads

beading cord and tie both ends together in a secure knot.

10. Strands 4 and 5: Repeat steps 4 to 6 and then 1 to 3, in that order, while stringing the beading cord through the fourth and fifth holes in the spacer bars.

I recommend working straight from the spool of elastic beading cord when you make this bracelet. I find this method is more convenient and cuts down on wasted beading cord.

Café-Au-Lait Bracelet

The rich colors and smooth textures of the beads in this bracelet make it a perfect accessory for an afternoon coffee date.

FINISHED MEASUREMENT

TOOLS

SKILL LEVEL

7½" (19 cm)

Wire cutters
Round-nose pliers

MATERIALS
52 beads, various shapes and colors, up to 10 mm
52 gold-plated eye pins, 2.5 cm
1 gold-plated 4-strand slide lock clasp

(continued on page 46)

(continued from page 44)

1. Divide the beads into 4 groups and arrange each group in a line this is even in length. The number of beads in each line may vary but the lengths should be even.

2. String 1 bead onto an eye pin and trim the eye pin to ⅜" (1 cm). Make a loop in the eye pin, but don't close the loop. Put the bead back in its place in the arrangement, then string the next bead onto an eye pin and repeat the process.

3. When all of the beads have been strung onto eye pins, connect one line of beads by drawing the open loop in each bead through the closed loop in the adjacent eye pin. Close the open loops.

4. Repeat step 3 to connect all of the beads in the line.

5. Open the loop at one end of one chain and string it through the rightmost loop on one half of the clasp. Close the loop.

6. Measure the chain of beads around your wrist to make sure it is the desired length. If it isn't quite right, add or remove beads as required.

7. When the chain is the right length, open the loop at the other end and string it through the rightmost loop on the other half of the clasp. Close the loop.

8. Repeat steps 3 to 5 to make the other 3 chains of beads. Measure these chains alongside the first chain to make sure they are even in length.

9. Attach the chains in adjacent and corresponding loops on both clasp halves.

Materials

Connect the beads through the loops in the eye pins

*When making
the loops in the
eye pins, try
to make them
even in size to
the original eye
pin loops. This
technique takes
a bit practice
but the result is
worth it.*

Connect one end of the bead
chain to half of the clasp

Measure the chain then connect
the other clasp half

Be-my-Valentine Bracelet

Memory wire makes light work of beaded jewelry,
since you don't need any crimp beads, clasps or jump rings.
All you need is a handful or two of beautiful beads.

FINISHED MEASUREMENT　　　　**TOOLS**　　　　**SKILL LEVEL**

3" (7.5 cm)

Round-nose pliers
Wire cutters
Flat-nose pliers

MATERIALS

4 turns of stainless steel memory wire, bracelet length
55 large beads, various colors and shapes, 5 to 10 mm
56 transparent gold seed beads, 5°
2 gold-plated jump rings, 4 mm
2 gold-plated charms, ⅜" (1 cm)
2 gold-plated head pins, 2.5 cm

(continued on page 50)

(continued from page 48)

1. Make a loop at one end of the memory wire.

2. Plan your arrangement of beads in any order you like. Integrate gold charms and bead caps as desired.

3. When you are satisfied with the arrangement of beads, start stringing them onto the memory wire. String on a seed bead between each large bead.

4. Continue stringing beads onto the memory wire until you have about ⅜" (1 cm) of bare wire left at the end. Make a loop in the memory wire, to secure the beads.

5. String a charm or large bead onto each head pin. Trim the head pin to ⅜" (1 cm) and make a loop at the end. String one head pin onto the loop on each end of the bracelet and close the loop.

Materials

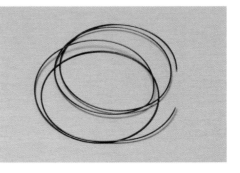

Make a loop at one end of the memory wire

Memory wire is available in various diameters. Copy this pattern using memory wire for a necklace, anklet or ring to make a simple set of jewelry.

Arrange the beads in a random pattern

String a seed bead after every large bead

Leather Cornucopia Necklace

In this design, the pearls and crystals evoke
a sense of classic beauty while the leather cord radiates hipness.
The combination is distinct and striking.

FINISHED MEASUREMENT	TOOLS	SKILL LEVEL

20" (51 cm)

Scissors
Flat-nose pliers
Wire cutters
Round-nose pliers

MATERIALS

120" (305 cm) leather cord, 1 mm
20 gold-plated crimp beads, 1 mm
15 white potato pearls, 6 mm
15 light pink oval faceted crystal beads, 5 mm
30 delicate bronze ball tip head pins, 2.5 cm
30 delicate bronze delicate jump rings, 4 mm
2 gold-plated cord tips, 5 mm
2 gold-plated jump rings, 5 mm
1 gold-plated clasp

Extension chain
2" (5 cm) gold-plated, small-link chain
1 gold-plated head pin, 2.5 cm
1 round faceted crystal bead, 4 mm

(continued on page 54)

(continued from page 52)

1. Cut the cord into six 20" (51 cm) pieces. String 5 crimp beads onto each piece of cord and position the beads at regular intervals along the cord. Make sure the beads are positioned at different intervals along each cord so that when the cords are gathered in a bunch, the crimp beads on each cord are visible.

2. When you are satisfied with the arrangement, flatten the crimp beads.

3. Gather the cords together and insert one end of all the cords into a cord tip; then flatten the cord tip.

4. Wrap one end of a piece of sewing thread several times around the burnt edge of the ribbon until the ribbon is small enough to fit through the bead holes.

5. String the free end of the sewing thread through the eye of the needle. Use the needle to string one group of beads onto the ribbon.

6. Repeat step 5 with the crystal beads.

7. Open a jump ring and string on one of the head pins from step 5. String the jump ring onto the leather cords, draw the jump ring down towards the knot you made in step 4, and close the jump ring.

8. When all the beads are attached, draw the beads towards the knot and measure 5½" (14 cm) from the other end of the necklace. Tie an overhand knot in the cords, so that the beads and crystals are concentrated in the center of the necklace.

9. Insert the other end of the necklace into a cord tip and flatten the cord tip.

10. Open both 5 mm jump rings and attach one at each end of the necklace. String the clasp onto one of the jump rings and close the jump rings.

Materials

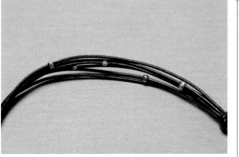

Position 5 crimp beads on each piece of cord

Connect each decorated head pin with a jump ring

11. Extension chain: String one end of the chain onto the other jump ring and close the jump ring. String the 5 mm crystal bead onto the 2.5 cm head pin and trim the head pin to ⅜" (1 cm). Make a loop in the head pin, draw it through the last link in the chain and close the loop.

There is no need to measure the intervals between crimp beads on the cords in this design. Just make sure the crimp beads are evenly distributed along each cord before flattening them.

Gather the beads and crystals at the center

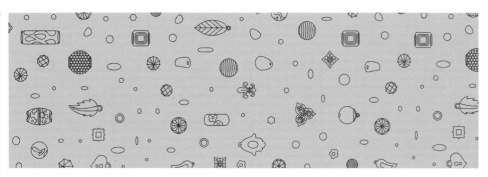

Innovative Organza Necklace

If you are looking to use something other than ordinary
beading thread for your next project, organza ribbon is an excellent alternative.
It's flexible enough to string beads and delicately holds them in place.

FINISHED MEASUREMENT	TOOLS	SKILL LEVEL
21" (53 cm)	*Scissors* *Lighter* *Needle* *Flat-nose pliers* *Round-nose pliers*	

MATERIALS

21 beads, assorted colors and shapes, up to 12 mm
57" (145 cm) light green organza ribbon, 1 cm
Sewing thread
2 antique gold cord tips, 5 mm
2 antique gold jump rings, 5 mm
1 gold-plated clasp

(continued on page 58)

(continued from page 56)

1. Divide the beads into 3 groups and arrange the beads in each group in adjacent rows. Make sure similar beads are neither side by side in the same row nor close together in adjacent rows.

2. Cut the ribbon into three 19" (48 cm) pieces.

3. Hold the end of one piece of ribbon and scorch it with a lighter to prevent the ribbon from fraying. Make sure you only scorch the edge of the ribbon.

4. Wrap sewing thread several times around the burnt edge of the ribbon to make it small enough to fit through the bead holes. Use a needle to help string the beads onto the ribbon if you like.

5. String a group of beads onto the ribbon. When all of the beads are strung, remove the sewing thread from the end.

6. Repeat steps 3 to 5 with the other two pieces of ribbon and groups of beads.

7. Gather one end of all three ribbons and tuck them into a cord tip. Flatten the cord tip to secure the ribbons.

8. Arrange the beads on each ribbon so that they are equidistant from each other. When the ribbons are placed alongside each other, make sure there are spaces between the beads on each ribbon.

9. Gather the other end of all 3 ribbons and tuck them into the other cord tip. Flatten the cord tip.

10. Open both jump rings and string each jump ring through the loop in each cord tip. String one of the jump rings through the loop on the clasp. Close both jump rings.

Materials

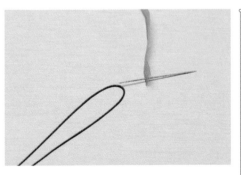

Use the needle to string beads onto the organza ribbon

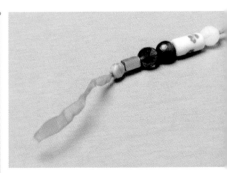

String one group of beads onto a ribbon

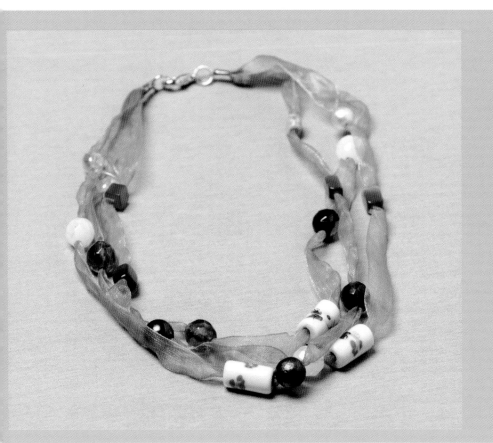

· When selecting the beads for this project, make sure the bead holes are big enough to fit over the organza ribbon, but small enough so that the beads stay in place after being positioned on the ribbon. ·

Gather one end of all three ribbons into cord tip

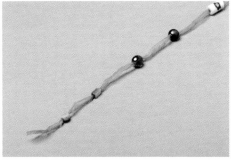

Distribute the beads evenly along each ribbon

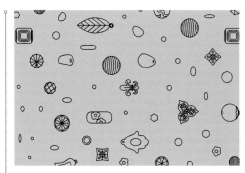

Stunningly Simple Drop Necklace

You don't need many crystals to make this pretty necklace.
I recommend selecting crystals of high quality
to make the most of their sparkle.

FINISHED MEASUREMENT　　　**TOOLS**　　　**SKILL LEVEL**

Necklace: 16½" (42 cm)
Pendant: 1½" (4 cm)

Wire cutters
Flat-nose pliers
Round-nose pliers

MATERIALS

19" (48 cm) delicate gold-plated small-link chain
4 rose bicone crystal beads, 6 mm
3 fuchsia bicone crystal beads, 6 mm
7 gold-plated eye pins, 2 cm
1 fuchsia teardrop crystal bead, 6 mm
1 gold-plated head pin, 2.5 cm
2 gold-plated jump rings, 5 mm
1 gold-plated lobster claw clasp

(continued on page 62)

(continued from page 60)

1. Cut the chain into 9 pieces, in the following lengths: two x 6" (15 cm); four x 1" (2.5 cm); three x ⅜" (1 cm).

2. String each bicone crystal bead onto an eye pin. Trim the eye pins to ⅜" (1 cm) and make a loop. Don't close the loop.

3. Connect the crystal beads and chain pieces in the following order: one 6" (15 cm) chain, 1 rose crystal bead, one 1" (2.5 cm) chain, 1 fuchsia bicone crystal bead, one 1" (2.5 cm) chain. Close the loops in the eye pins to connect the elements.

4. Repeat step 3 to make a second chain of beads and chains.

5. Connect the two chains you made in steps 3 and 4 at one end by stringing the free end of both 1" (2.5 cm) chains through the loop at the top of 1 rose crystal bead. Close the loop.

6. Attach the following chains and beads to the rose bead you attached in step 5: one ⅜" (1 cm) chain, 1 fuchsia crystal bead, one ⅜" (1 cm) chain, 1 rose crystal bead, one ⅜" (1 cm) chain.

7. String the fuchsia teardrop crystal bead onto the head pin. Trim the wire to ⅜" (1 cm) and make a loop. String the loop through the bottom link in the last chain you connected in step 6 and close the loop.

8. Open both jump rings and string each one through the link at either end of the necklace. String the clasp onto one of the jump rings. Close the jump rings

Materials

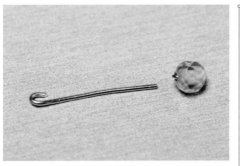

String each crystal bead onto an eye pin

Connect the crystal beads with pieces of chain

To make a bolder version of this necklace, replace the delicate chain with something sturdier and use larger crystal beads. You might need to choose longer eye pins as well.

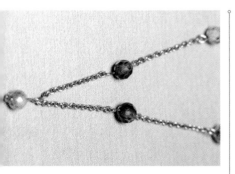

Connect the sides of the necklace with a rose crystal

Connect a fuchsia crystal to the rose crystal

Darling Dangling Necklace

This necklace features dozens of beads, in various colors and sizes, strung onto a gold-plated chain. It's a great design for using leftover beads from another project.

FINISHED MEASUREMENT	TOOLS	SKILL LEVEL

20" (50 cm)

Flat-nose pliers
Round-nose pliers
Wire cutters

MATERIALS

19" (48 cm) gold-plated round cable-link chain
46 gold-plated head pins, 2.5 cm
46 beads, various colors and shapes, up to 8 mm
2 gold-plated jump rings, 5 mm
1 gold-plated lobster claw clasp

(continued on page 66)

(continued from page 64)

1. Lay the chain on your work surface and arrange the beads alongside of it until you find a composition that you like. I recommend positioning the larger beads first, so that they are evenly dispersed along the length of the chain, then placing the smaller beads in between.

2. When you are satisfied with the bead arrangement, begin stringing the beads onto head pins. Trim each headpin to ⅜" (1 cm) and make a loop. Don't close the loop.

3. String the beads onto the links in the chain via the loop at the top of the head pin bead. Close the loop to secure the bead.

4. Open both jump rings and string one at either end of the chain. String the clasp onto one of the jump rings. Close both jump rings.

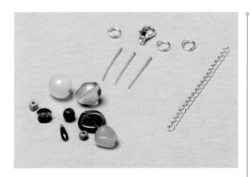

Materials

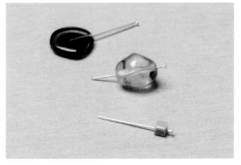

String each bead onto a head pin

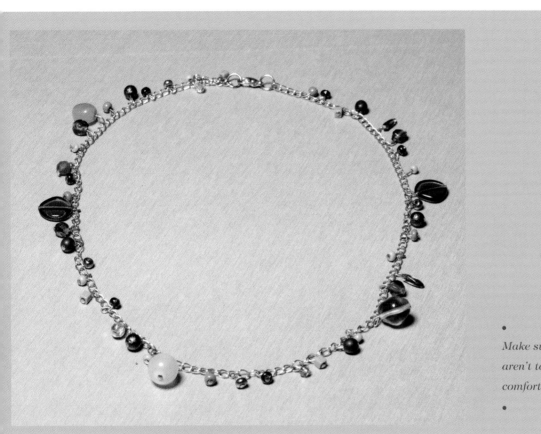

Make sure the links in your chain aren't too small so that you can comfortably string on the head pins.

First position the larger beads, and then the smaller ones

Use jump rings to attach the clasp

Queen of the Rings Necklace

This dramatic necklace is perfect for an evening
at the opera, the theater or any other affair.

FINISHED MEASUREMENT   TOOLS   SKILL LEVEL

17¾" (45 cm)

Wire cutters
Flat-nose pliers
Round-nose pliers

MATERIALS

100" (250 cm) nylon-coated stainless steel beading wire, 0.022" (0.55 mm)
20 gold-plated crimp beads
50 grams black 2-cut seed beads, 11°
3 gold-plated jump rings, 5 mm
1 gold-plated textured hoop, 3.5 cm diameter
1 gold-plated textured hoop, 3 cm diameter
1 gold-plated textured hoop, 2 cm diameter
1 gold-plated clasp

(continued on page 70)

(continued from page 68)

1. Cut a 20" (50 cm) piece of beading wire.

2. String 2 crimp beads onto one end of the wire. Make a loop at the end of the beading wire and tuck the tip back into the crimp beads. Flatten the crimp beads.

3. String seed beads onto the beading wire until the beaded length is about 17" (43 cm). String 2 crimp beads onto the beading wire and make a loop at the end. Tuck the tip of the wire back into the crimp beads and flatten the crimp beads.

4. Repeat steps 1 to 3 another four times.

5. Open 1 jump ring and string it through the loops at one end of all 5 beaded chains. Close the jump ring.

6. Open 1 jump ring and string it through the loops at the other end of all 5 beaded chains. String the clasp onto the jump ring; then close the jump ring.

7. Place the gold-plated hoops in a stack, with the largest hoop on the bottom. Open 1 jump ring and insert all three hoops. Insert the third beaded chain into the jump ring and close the jump ring.

Materials

String the beads onto the beading wire

Connect one end of all the beaded chain

This necklace uses jump rings rather than multi-strand connectors to connect all five strands. Select sturdy jump rings for this purpose and close them securely.

ttach a clasp to one end of the necklace

Use a jump ring to connect the large hoops

Striking Silver and Leather Necklace

Jump rings are often used as components but they can also be used as silver beads. In this necklace, dozens of them are used to make the pendant.

FINISHED MEASUREMENT   TOOLS   SKILL LEVEL

Necklace: 24" (61 cm)   *Scissors*
Pendant: 1½" (4 cm)   *Wire cutters*
                               Flat-nose pliers
                               Round-nose pliers

MATERIALS

31" (79 cm) black leather cord, 2 mm   *Extension chain*
4 silver-plated cord tips, 2 mm   *2" (5 cm) silver-plated, small-link chain*
56 thick silver-plated jump rings, 1 cm   *1 black crystal bead, 5 mm*
1 transparent round crystal bead, 12 mm   *1 silver-plated head pin, 2.5 cm*
1 silver-plated head pin, 3.5 cm
8 silver-plated crimp beads, 2.5 mm
2 silver-plated jump rings, 5 mm
1 silver-plated lobster claw clasp

(continued on page 74)

(continued from page 72)

1. Cut the leather cord into two pieces: 1 x 4" (10 cm) and 1 x 27" (69 cm).

2. To make the pendant, tuck each end of the 4" (10 cm) piece of leather cord into a cord tip. Flatten the cord tips.

3. Set aside one 1 cm jump ring and string the rest onto the cord. The cord will be crowded, so hold both ends in your hand to make sure the jump rings don't slip off.

4. Open one 5 mm jump ring and string it through both cord tips. Close the jump ring. Now you'll have a leather loop of rings for the pendant.

5. To make the necklace, fold the 27" (69 cm) piece of leather in half and draw the folded end through the remaining 1 cm jump ring. Make a lark's knot to connect the leather cord to the jump ring.

6. Open the jump ring and string it through three of the rings on the pendant. Close the jump ring.

7. String the 12 mm crystal bead onto the 3.5 cm head pin and trim the head pin to ⅜" (1 cm). Make a loop in the head pin and attach it to a jump ring at the top of the pendant. Close the jump ring.

8. String 1 crimp bead onto the leather cord and draw it along until it is about 2" (5 cm) from the pendant. Flatten the crimp bead. String 3 more crimp beads onto this side of the leather cord and position them at 2" (5 cm) intervals. Flatten the crimp beads.

9. Repeat step 8 on the other side of the leather cord.

10. Tuck each end of the leather cord into a cord tip. Flatten the cord tips. Open two 5 mm jump rings and string one through each cord tip. String the clasp onto one of the jump rings and close the jump ring.

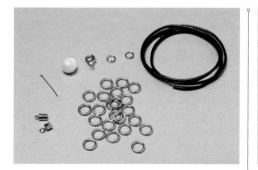

Materials

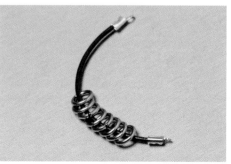

String jump rings onto the short piece of leather cord

Secure the ring of jump rings using a jump ring

11. Extension chain: String one end of the chain onto the other jump ring and close the jump ring. String the 5 mm crystal bead onto the 2.5 cm head pin and trim the head pin to ³⁄₈" (1 cm). Make a loop in the head pin, draw it through the last link in the chain and close the loop.

When making the pendant, it's easy stringing jump rings onto the leather cord but a bit harder keeping them in place! If you can't hold the cord ends together on your own, ask someone for help.

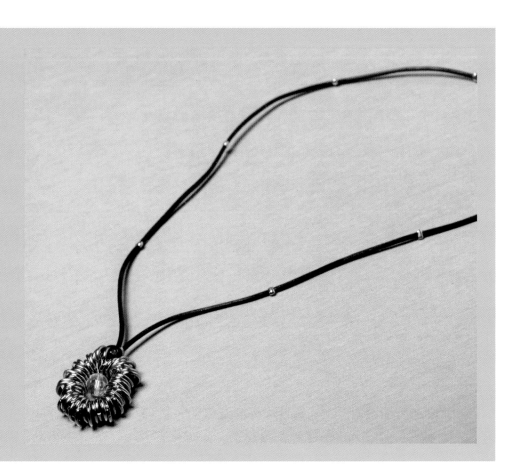

Attach the crystal bead to the middle of the pendant

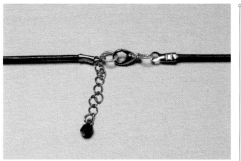

Add an extension chain for flexible sizing

Chunky Turquoise Chip Necklace

Turquoise chips are excellent for making unique jewelry,
since no two pieces are alike. In this design, these bright
beads are collected in the middle of the necklace.

FINISHED MEASUREMENT	TOOLS	SKILL LEVEL
20" (51 cm)	Scissors Flat-nose pliers Round-nose pliers	

MATERIALS

16" (40 cm) brown bolo cord, 2 mm

4 gold-plated cord tips, 2 mm

4 gold-plated jump rings, 5 mm

4 gold-plated crimp beads, 1.5 mm

5" (13 cm) nylon-coated, stainless steel beading wire, 0.022" (0.55 mm)

30 turquoise chip beads (enough to fill 4" (10 cm) of wire), side-to-side, top-drilled, various lengths

1 gold-plated lobster claw clasp

Extension chain

2" (5 cm) gold-plated small-link chain

1 turquoise faceted crystal bead, 5 mm

1 gold-plated head pin, 2.5 cm

(continued on page 78)

(continued from page 76)

1. Cut the bolo cord into two 8" (20 cm) pieces. Insert each end of each piece into a cord tip and flatten the cord tips.

2. Open 2 jump rings and string one of them onto one of the cord tips on each bolo cord. Close the jump rings.

3. String 2 crimp beads onto the beading wire. Draw the tip of the wire through one of the jump rings you secured in step 2, and then back into the crimp beads. Flatten the crimp beads.

4. Arrange the turquoise beads on your work surface until you are satisfied with their composition. String the beads onto the beading wire until 4" (10 cm) of wire are beaded.

5. String 2 crimp beads onto the other end of the beading wire; then draw the tip of the wire through a jump ring on the other cord. Insert the tip back into the crimp beads and flatten the crimp beads.

6. Open 2 jump rings and string each one onto the free end on each cord. Attach the clasp to one of the jump rings and close the jump ring.

7. Extension chain: String one end of the chain onto the other jump ring and close the jump ring. String the crystal bead on the head pin and trim the head pin to ⅜" (1 cm). Make a loop in the head pin, draw it through the last link in the chain and close the loop.

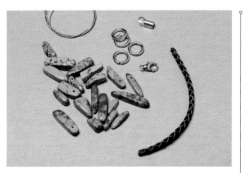

Materials

Attach a cord tip to either end of the bolo cord

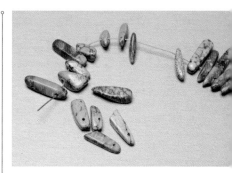

String turquoise chip beads onto the beading wire

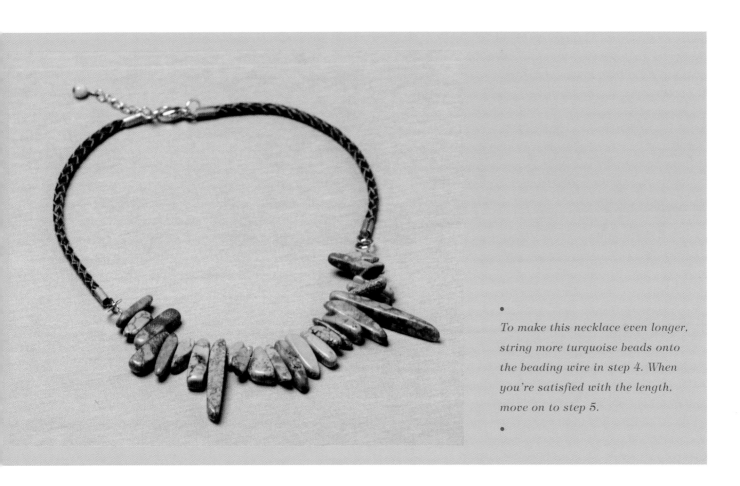

To make this necklace even longer, string more turquoise beads onto the beading wire in step 4. When you're satisfied with the length, move on to step 5.

Attach the beading wire to the bolo cord

Attach a clasp to finish the necklace

Flower Power Necklace

Make your very own flowers with this intricate design.
Don't be deceived by the delicate appearance of this piece
—it's actually made using wire!

FINISHED MEASUREMENT	TOOLS	SKILL LEVEL

Necklace: 20" (50 cm)
Pendant: 4¾" (12 cm)

Wire cutters
Flat-nose pliers
Round-nose pliers

MATERIALS

83" (210 cm) half-hard copper wire, 24 gauge (0.5 mm)
58 light turquoise faceted crystal beads, 7 mm
27 pale yellow faceted crystal beads, 5 mm
1 gold-plated leaf charm, 15 mm
8 gold-plated jump rings, 5 mm
12" (30 cm) nylon-coated, stainless steel beading wire, 0.022" (0.55 mm)
8 gold-plated crimp beads, 1.5 mm

Extension chain

2" (5 cm) copper small-link chain
1 pale yellow faceted crystal bead, 5 mm
1 copper head pin, 2.5 cm

(continued on page 82)

(continued from page 80)

1. Cut three 4" (10 cm) pieces of wire. Twist one end of the wires together to form a twisted tail that is about 1" (2.5 cm) long. You'll be using this tail later to make a loop. Separate the wires about the twisted area into a 3-pronged fork.

2. String 2 turquoise beads onto the top wire, 1 turquoise, 1 pale yellow and 1 turquoise bead onto the middle wire, and 2 turquoise beads onto the bottom wire.

3. Bring all three wires together and arrange the beads to form a flower shape. Twist the wires together several times at this end of the flower

to form a twisted tail that is about 1" (2.5 cm). Form a loop at this end of the flower.

4. Form a loop at the other end of the flower as well.

5. Repeat steps 1 to 4 to make two more flowers with turquoise petals and pale yellow centers. Repeat another 3 times to make 3 flowers with pale yellow petals and turquoise centers.

6. Open 1 jump ring and use it to connect 1 pale yellow flower and 1 turquoise flower.

7. Repeat step 6 once.

8. Open 2 jump rings and use them to connect 1 pale yellow flower, 1 turquoise flower and 1 pale yellow flower in a chain. Open 1 jump ring and use it to connect the leaf charm to the end of the chain.

9. Open 1 jump ring and use it to connect the turquoise flowers on the 2-flower chains and the pale yellow flower at the top of the 3-flower chain to make a Y shape. Close the jump ring.

10. Cut the beading wire into two 6" (15 cm) pieces.

Materials

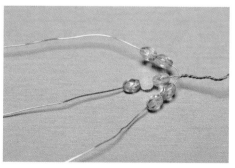

Separate the wires and string on the beads

Twist the wires together above the flower

11. String 2 crimp beads onto one piece of beading wire and string the end of the wire into the loop at the free end of one pale yellow flower. Tuck the tip of the wire back into the crimp beads and flatten the crimp beads.

12. String 18 turquoise beads onto the wire, then string on 2 crimp beads. Make a loop at the end of the wire and tuck the tip back into the crimp beads. Flatten the crimp beads.

13. Repeat steps 11 and 12 on the other side of the necklace.

14. Open 2 jump rings and string one through the loop at each end of the necklace. String the clasp onto one of the jump rings and close the jump ring.

15. Extension chain: String one end of the chain onto the other jump ring and close the jump ring. String the crystal bead on the head pin and trim the head pin to ⅜" (1 cm). Make a loop in the head pin, draw it through the last link in the chain and close the loop.

Try to make the beaded flowers similar in size for this design. If one or two flowers are larger than the rest, use them to make the pendant.

Form a loop at both ends of the flower

Connect the flowers to each other using jump rings

Connect 3 flowers in a Y shape to attach the pendant

Enviably Green Necklace

This design is great if you want to make a necklace that is just right for a specific outfit. Simply select a handful of beads that match and choose your favorite type of metallic chain and findings.

FINISHED MEASUREMENT	TOOLS	SKILL LEVEL
18" (46 cm)	*Flat-nose pliers*	
	Round-nose pliers	
	Wire cutters	

MATERIALS

9 round beads, various shades of green and gold, 6 to 10 mm

4 copper bead caps, 8 mm

17" (43 cm) copper small-link chain

18 transparent gold seed beads, 6°

18 copper crimp beads, 1.5 mm

2 copper cord tips, 1 mm

1 copper clasp

2 copper jump rings, 5 mm

Extension chain

2" (5 cm) copper small-link chain

1 copper head pin, 5 mm

1 small crystal bead, 5 mm

(continued on page 86)

(continued from page 84)

1. Arrange the round beads in a line on your work surface until you are satisfied with the order. Position bead caps around two of the beads.

2. String the middle bead in the arrangement onto the chain and draw it along to the middle of the chain.

3. String a seed bead onto each end of the chain and draw the beads along until they reach the middle bead.

4. String a crimp bead onto each end of the chain and draw each bead along until it reaches the seed beads sandwiching the middle bead. Make sure the middle bead is in the right position and the seed beads and crimp beads are flush on either side; then flatten the crimp beads.

5. String a crimp bead onto one end of the chain and draw it along until it is 1½" (3.8 cm) from one of the flattened crimp beads. Flatten the crimp bead. String on a seed bead, the next round bead in your arrangement, a seed bead and a crimp bead. Make sure the beads are flush against the flattened crimp bead and then flatten the crimp bead.

6. Repeat step 5 to string 3 more round beads, sandwiched by seed beads and crimp beads, onto this side of the necklace. Repeat again to string 4 round beads onto the other side of the necklace.

7. Insert each end of the chain into a cord tip and flatten the cord tips.

8. Open 2 jump rings and string one through each cord tip. String the clasp onto one of the jump rings and close the jump ring.

Materials

Sandwich each large bead between 2 seed beads

Leave even intervals between each cluster of beads

9. Extension chain: String one end of the 2" (5 cm) chain onto the other jump ring and close the jump ring. String the 5 mm crystal bead onto the 2.5 cm head pin and trim the head pin to ⅜" (1 cm). Make a loop in the head pin, draw it through the last link in the chain and close the loop.

For evenly spaced bead clusters, cut a 1½" (3.8 cm) piece of cardboard and use this to measure the intervals between each cluster.

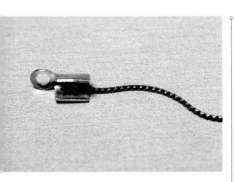

nsert each end of the chain into a cord tip

Use jump rings to attach the clasp

Cleopatra's Crystal Necklace

This dramatic necklace is sure to evoke comments
and compliments. It takes a bit of time and planning to make,
but the results are worth it. Fit for a queen.

FINISHED MEASUREMENT

TOOLS

SKILL LEVEL

Shortest chain: 14" (35.5 cm)
Longest chain: 15" (38 cm)

Scissors
Flat-nose pliers
Wire cutters
Round-nose pliers

MATERIALS

100" (250 cm) nylon-coated, stainless steel beading
wire, 0.022" (0.55 mm)
20 gold-plated crimp beads, 1.5 mm
2 gold-plated 4-loop connector bars
15 grams transparent gold beads, 11°
2 gold-plated 5-loop spacer bars
30 grams transparent gold beads, 6°
201 pale yellow bicone crystals, 5 mm
28 antiqued gold rondelle beads, 5 mm

17 decorated metallic gold round beads, 5 mm
2 gold-plated jump rings
1 gold-plated clasp

Extension chain
2" (5 cm) gold-plated, small-link chain
1 gold-plated head pin, 2.5 cm
1 pale yellow crystal bead, 5 mm

(continued on page 90)

(continued from page 88)

1. Strand 1: Cut a 20" (51 cm) piece of beading wire and string on 2 crimp beads. Draw the tip of the wire through the first hole in one of the connector bars and make a loop in the tip; then draw the wire back into the crimp beads. Flatten the crimp beads.

2. String 11° gold seed beads onto the beading wire for 1½" (4 cm), then draw the wire through the first hole in a spacer bar.

3. String 11° gold seed beads for another 11" (28 cm), then draw the beading wire through the first hole in the other spacer bar. String another 1½" (4 cm) of 11° gold seed beads,

then string on 2 crimp beads. Draw the tip of the beading wire through the first hole in the other connector bar. Make a loop at the tip of the beading wire and insert it back into the crimp beads. Flatten the crimp beads.

4. Strand 2: Repeat step 1 to connect another piece of beading wire to the first hole in the first connector bar.

5. String 6° gold seed beads onto the wire for 1½" (4 cm), then draw the wire through the second hole in the first spacer bar.

6. Repeat steps 2 and 3 using 6° gold seed beads and stringing the beading wire through the second hole in the other spacer bar and the first hole in the second connector bar.

7. Strand 3: Repeat step 1 to connect a piece of beading wire to the second hole in the first connector bar. String on 2 pale yellow crystal beads, 1 rondelle bead, 2 pale yellow crystal beads, 1 rondelle bead and 2 pale yellow crystal beads.

8. Draw the wire through the third hole in the spacer bar, then string a pattern of 2 pale yellow crystal beads and 1 rondelle bead for 11 ⅗" (29.5 cm).

Materials

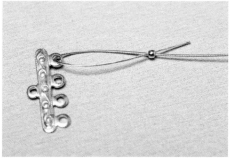

Attach a piece of beading wire to the first connector hole

String on a pattern of crystal and gold beads

9. Draw the wire through the third hole in the other spacer bar and repeat the pattern of beads from step 7 for 1½" (4 cm). String 2 crimp beads onto the beading wire and secure the wire to the second hole in the second connector bar.

10. Strand 4: Repeat step 1 to connect a piece of beading wire to the third hole in the first connector bar. String on 3 pale yellow crystal beads, 1 decorated metallic gold round bead and 3 pale yellow crystal beads. String the beading wire through the fourth hole in the spacer bar, then string a pattern of 3 pale

yellow crystal beads and 1 decorated metallic gold bead for 12" (30.5 cm).

11. Strand 5: Repeat step 1 to connect the last piece of beading wire to the fourth hole in the first connector bar. String pale yellow crystal beads for 1½" (4 cm) then draw the beading wire through the fifth hole in the spacer bar.

12. String pale yellow crystal beads for 12 ⅖" (31.5 cm); then draw the beading wire through the fifth hole in the second spacer bar. String pale yellow crystal beads for 1½" (4 cm); then attach the beading wire to the fourth hole in the second connector bar.

13. Open both jump rings and attach one to each connector bar. Affix the clasp to one jump ring and close the jump ring.

14. Extension chain: String one end of the chain onto the other jump ring and close the jump ring. String the 5 mm crystal bead onto the 2.5 cm head pin and trim the head pin to ⅜" (1 cm). Make a loop in the head pin, draw it through the last link in the chain and close the loop.

Securely attach the beaded wires with crimp beads

Finished

The trick to making this necklace hang properly is making sure each strand is slightly longer than the previous one. Check the way each strand hangs before securing it with crimp beads.

Twinkling Triple Turquoise Necklace

This necklace is bright and colorful an easy-to-wear accessory for any outfit.
Replace some of the large crystal beads with a few 6° seed beads.
Use a different color of seed beads for a completely different look!

FINISHED MEASUREMENT	TOOLS	SKILL LEVEL

Shortest chain: 15 ¾" (40 cm)
Longest chain: 18 ½" (47 cm)

Wire cutters
Flat-nose pliers
Round-nose pliers

MATERIALS

60" (150 cm) nylon-coated, stainless steel beading wire, 0.022" (0.55 mm)
12 silver-plated crimp beads, 1.5 mm
2 silver-plated 3-loop connector bars
50 grams turquoise seed beads, 11°
50 crystal beads, various colors, 8 to 10 mm
2 silver-plated jump rings, 5 mm
1 silver-plated clasp

Extension chain

2" (5 cm) silver-plated, small-link chain
1 black crystal bead, 5 mm
1 silver-plated head pin, 2.5 cm

(continued on page 94)

(continued from page 92)

1. Cut a 15¾" (40 cm) piece of beading wire. String 2 crimp beads onto one end of a piece of beading wire and draw the tip of the wire through the first loop on one connector bar. Tuck the tip back into the crimp beads and flatten the crimp beads.

2. String 11 seed beads, 1 crystal bead, 11 seed beads and 1 crystal onto the beading wire.

3. Repeat step 2 until 14½" (37 cm) of beading wire are beaded. String 2 crimp beads onto the end of the beading wire then string the tip of the wire through the first loop on the other connector bar. Tuck the tip back

into the crimp beads and flatten the crimp beads.

4. Cut a 17½" (44.5 cm) piece of beading wire and attach it to the second loop on the bar, using 2 crimp beads as you did in step 1.

5. Repeat step 2 until 16" (40.6 cm) of beading wire have been beaded; then connect this end of the wire to the second loop on the other connector bar, using 2 crimp beds.

6. Cut a 23½" (57 cm) piece of beading wire and attach it to the third loop on the connector bar. Repeat step 2 until 17¾" (45 cm) of the wire

have been beaded; then connect the other end of the wire to the third loop in the connector bar.

7. Open both jump rings and string one through each connector bar. String the clasp onto one of the jump rings and close the jump ring.

8. String one end of the 2" (5 cm) chain onto the other jump ring and close the jump ring.

9. Extension chain: String the 5 mm crystal bead onto the head pin and trim the head pin to ⅜" (1 cm). Make a loop in the head pin, draw it through the last link in the chain and close the loop.

Materials

String 11 seed beads between each crystal bead

Securely attach the beaded wires with crimp beads

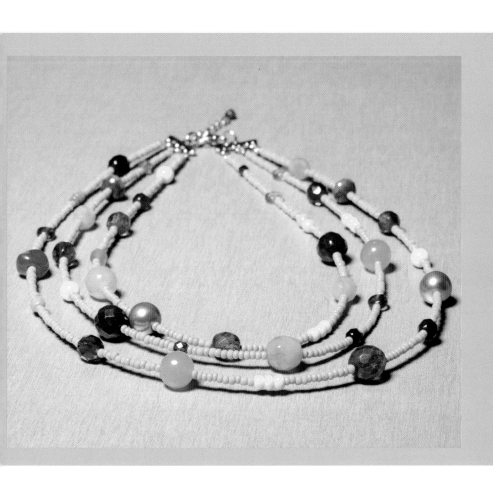

Each strand in this necklace is a different length. For a more dramatic design, make the second and third strands even longer.

Bright Blue Beaded Necklace

With its simple yet classy appearance,
this necklace is just right for wearing
to the office or an evening on the town.

FINISHED MEASUREMENT

TOOLS

SKILL LEVEL

17¾" (45 cm)

Wire cutters
Flat-nose pliers
Round-nose pliers

MATERIALS
13 royal blue glass disk beads, 15 mm
13 gold-plated eye pins, 3 cm
7" (18 cm) gold-plated, large-link chain
4 gold-plated jump rings, 5 mm
2 gold-plated jump rings, 7 mm
1 gold-plated clasp

Extension chain
2" (5 cm) gold-plated, small-link chain
1 gold-plated head pin, 2.5 cm
1 crystal bead, 4 mm

(continued on page 98)

(continued from page 96)

1. String a glass bead onto an eye pin. Trim the eye pin to ⅜" (1 cm) and make a loop. Do not close the loop.

2. Repeat step 1 to string all the glass beads onto eye pins.

3. Connect 1 glass bead to another by stringing the open loop at the end of one bead through the closed loop at the end of another bead. Close the loop.

4. Repeat step 3 to make two chains of 4 beads and one chain of 5 beads.

5. Separate the chain into two pieces, one measuring 4" (10 cm) (4 links) and one measuring about 5" (13 cm) (5 links).

6. Open the 5 mm jump rings and use them to connect the chains of beads to the gold-plated chains in the following order: one 4-bead chain, one 5-link chain, one 5-bead chain, one 4-link chain, one 4-bead chain.

7. Open both 7 mm jump rings and attach one at each end of the necklace. String the clasp onto one of the jump rings; then close the jump ring.

8. Extension chain: String one end of the 2" (5 cm) chain onto the other jump ring and close the jump ring. String the crystal bead onto the 2.5 cm head pin and trim the head pin to ⅜" (1 cm). Make a loop in the head pin, draw it through the last link in the chain and close the loop.

Materials

Attach the glass beads through the eye pin loops

Attach the glass beads to the link chain

The links in this chain have a diameter of about 10 mm. If the links in your chain are smaller or larger, increase or decrease the number of links you place between each cluster of disk beads.

Super Hoop Necklace

This striking design is a wonderful way
to show off a special hoop or pendant.
Perfect with an open-neck shirt or tank top.

FINISHED MEASUREMENT

21" (51 cm)

TOOLS

Scissors
Flat-nose pliers
Round-nose pliers

SKILL LEVEL

MATERIALS

60" (152 cm) black wax-covered cotton cord, 0.8 mm
1 round ceramic hoop, 5 cm
4 textured brown beads, 10 mm
42 brown matte seed beads, 6°
36 yellow triangle beads, 6 mm
2 decorated yellow lampwork beads, 12 mm
2 antique copper cord tips, 3 mm
2 antique copper jump rings, 4 mm
1 copper lobster claw clasp

(continued on page 102)

(continued from page 100)

1. Cut the cord into three 20" (50 cm) pieces. Hold all 3 cords together and fold them in half. Draw the folded end of the cords through the ceramic hoop, then make a lark's knot with the cords to secure hoop.

2. Measure ¾" (2 cm) from one side of the pendant and tie an overhand knot with all three cords.

3. Repeat step 2 on the other side of the pendant.

4. String 1 textured brown bead onto 1 cord; then tie all 3 cords in a knot above the bead.

5. Separate the 3 cords, then string 1 seed bead, 1 triangle bead, 1 seed bead and 1 triangle bead onto one cord.

6. On each of the other 2 cords, string 1 triangle bead, 1 seed bead, 1 triangle bead and 1 seed bead. Tie all 3 cords together in an overhand knot.

7. String 1 decorated lampwork bead onto all 3 cords; then make an overhand knot in all three cords.

8. Repeat steps 5 and 6, then string 1 textured brown bead onto

one cord. Tie all 3 cords in an overhand knot and then repeat steps 5 and 6 again.

9. Repeat steps 4 to 8 on the other side of the necklace.

10. Insert each end of the necklace into a cord tip and flatten the cord tips. Open both jump rings and insert one jump ring into each cord tip. Attach the clasp to one of the jump rings and close the jump rings.

Materials

Make a lark's knot to connect the cords to the hoop

String a textured brown bead onto one cor

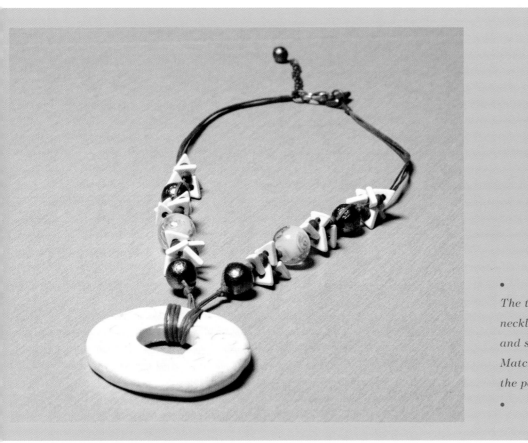

The technique used in this necklace can transform any large and striking hoop into a pendant. Match your beads to the color of the pendant you choose.

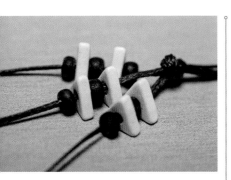

String triangle beads and seed beads onto each cord

String a lampwork bead onto all three cords

Finish the necklace with jump rings and a clasp

Charming Leather Necklace

This design combines soft leather cord with turquoise and gold beads.
It can be worn as a long or short necklace or
wrapped several times around the wrist as a bracelet.

FINISHED MEASUREMENT

42" (106 cm)

TOOLS

Scissors
Flat-nose pliers
Round-nose pliers
Wire cutters

SKILL LEVEL

MATERIALS

22 gold-plated crimp beads, 2 mm
42" (106 cm) brown leather cord, 2 mm
2 gold-plated cord tips, 2 mm
24 gold-plated jump rings, 3 mm
23–30 turquoise, gold and pearl beads, various sizes
10 gold-plated bead caps
23 gold-plated head pins, 2.5 cm
2 gold-plated jump rings, 6 mm
1 gold-plated clasp

Extension chain

2" (5 cm) gold-plated, small-link chain
1 gold-plated head pin, 2 cm
1 turquoise crystal bead, 4 mm

(continued on page 106)

(continued from page 104)

1. String a crimp bead onto the leather cord and draw it along until it is about 2" (5 cm) from one end of the cord. Flatten the crimp bead.

2. String another crimp bead onto the leather cord and draw it along until it is about 2" (5 cm) from the first crimp bead. Flatten the crimp bead.

3. Repeat step 2 until all crimp beads are located at even intervals along the leather cord.

4. String a cord tip onto each end of the leather cord and flatten.

5. Open one 3 mm jump ring and string it onto the leather cord, between the first cord tip and the first crimp bead. Open the rest of the 3 mm jump rings and position one between every two crimp beads. Open the remaining jump ring and position it between the last crimp bead and the last cord tip.

6. String each bead onto a head pin. If you are using bead caps, sandwich some of the beads with them. You can also replace some of the beads with small charms. Trim each head pin to ⅜" (1 cm) and make a closed loop.

7. String each head pin onto a jump ring; then close the loop in the jump ring.

8. Open both 6 mm jump rings and string one through each cord tip. Attach the clasp to one of the jump rings and close the jump ring.

9. Extension chain: String one end of the 2" (5 cm) chain onto the other jump ring and close the jump ring. String the 5 mm crystal bead onto the 2.5 cm head pin and trim the head pin to ⅜" (1 cm). Make a loop in the head pin, draw it through the last link in the chain and close the loop.

Materials

String crimp beads onto the leather cord

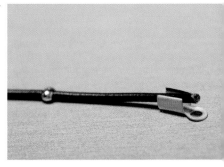

Tuck each end of the cord into a cord tip

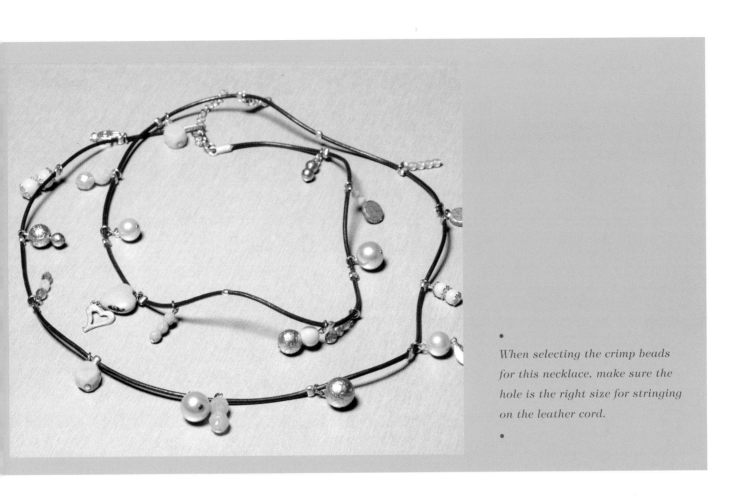

When selecting the crimp beads for this necklace, make sure the hole is the right size for stringing on the leather cord.

Positively Purple Pendant Necklace

Dress up a delicate gold chain with this sparkling collection
of purple charms, crystals and beads

FINISHED MEASUREMENT　　　　　**TOOLS**　　　　　**SKILL LEVEL**

20" (50 cm)

Wire cutters
Flat-nose pliers
Round-nose pliers

MATERIALS

1 rectangular 4-hole crystal setting, 20 x 10 mm
20" (51 cm) gold-plated, small-link chain
1 purple rectangular flat-back crystal, 20 x 10 mm
1 round purple bead, 5 mm
1 gold-plated head pin, 2 cm
3 gold-plated jump rings, 4 mm
1 gold-plated decorative hoop, 2 cm
1 gold-plated leaf charm, 2 cm
1 purple glass leaf charm, 2 cm

2 gold-plated cord tips, 2 mm
2 gold-plated jump rings, 5 mm
1 gold-plated clasp

Extension chain
2" (5 cm) gold-plated, small-link chain
1 gold-plated head pin, 2 mm
1 crystal bead, 4 mm

(continued on page 110)

(continued from page 108)

1. String the setting onto both ends of the chain and draw it down evenly along both sides of the chain.

2. Place the purple flat-back crystal in the setting and fold down the prongs to secure.

3. String the round purple crystal bead onto the head pin. Trim the head pin to ⅜" (1 cm) and make a loop. Don't close the loop. String the loop onto the chain below the flat-back crystal and close the loop.

4. Open a jump ring and string it through the decorative gold-plated loop.

5. String the jump ring onto the chain below the flat-back crystal and close the jump ring.

6. Repeat step 5 with the other gold leaf charm and the glass leaf charm.

7. Insert each end of the chain into a cord tip and flatten the cord tip. Open both 5 mm jump rings and string each one through a loop on a cord tip. String the clasp onto one of the jump rings and close the jump rings.

8. Extension chain: String one end of the chain onto the other jump ring and close the jump ring. String the 5 mm crystal bead onto the 2.5 cm head pin and trim the head pin to ⅜" (1 cm). Make a loop in the head pin, draw it through the last link in the chain and close the loop.

Materials

String the setting onto both ends of the chain

Secure the crystal in the setting by folding the prongs

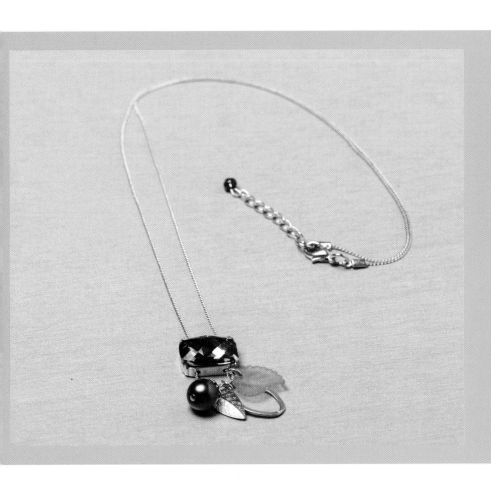

The rectangular crystal takes center stage in this piece, so choose one that really sparkles. As for the mounting, make sure it is of high quality.

Finished

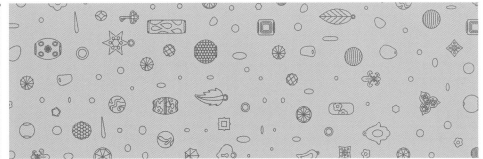

Starry Nights Necklace

This necklace evokes the beauty and romance of an impressionist painting.
It's a lovely design for showing off delicately decorated millefiori beads.

FINISHED MEASUREMENT

TOOLS

SKILL LEVEL

19" (48 cm)

Scissors
Flat-nose pliers
Round-nose pliers

MATERIALS

55" (140 cm) nylon-coated
stainless steel beading wire, 0.022" (0.55 mm)
60 silver-plated crimp beads, 1 mm
30 star-shaped millefiori glass beads, 10 mm
2 silver-plated cord tips, 3 mm
2 silver-plated jump rings, 5 mm
1 silver-plated clasp

Extension chain
2" (5 cm) silver-plated, small-link chain
1 silver-plated head pin, 2.5 cm
1 crystal bead, 4 mm

(continued on page 114)

(continued from page 112)

1. Cut the beading wire into three 18" (46 cm) pieces. String a crimp bead onto one end of one piece of wire and draw it along until it is 1¼" (3 cm) from the end. Flatten the bead. String a star-shaped bead onto the wire, then string on another crimp bead. Flatten the crimp bead.

2. String a crimp bead onto the wire and draw it along until it is 1" (2.5 cm) from the last crimp bead. Flatten the bead.

3. String a star-shaped bead onto the wire, then another crimp bead. Flatten the crimp bead.

4. Repeat steps 2 and 3 until 10 star beads have been strung onto the beading wire.

5. String a crimp bead onto another piece of beading wire. Draw the crimp bead along until it is 2" (5 cm) from the end of the wire and flatten the bead. String a star-shaped bead onto the wire, then string on another crimp bead. Flatten the crimp bead.

6. Repeat steps 2 and 3 to string a total of 10 star beads onto the beading wire.

7. String a crimp bead onto the third piece of beading wire and draw the crimp bead along until it is 1½" (4 cm) from the end of the wire and flatten the bead. String a star-shaped bead onto the wire, then string on another crimp bead. Flatten the crimp bead.

8. Repeat steps 2 and 3 until the last 10 star beads have been strung onto the wire.

9. Insert one end of all 3 wires into a cord tip and flatten the cord tip. Repeat at the other end.

10. Open both jump rings and insert one into each cord tip. String the clasp onto one of the jump rings and close the jump ring.

Materials

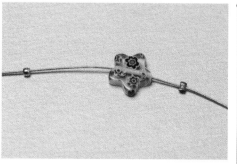

Sandwich each star-shaped bead with crimp beads

Leave even intervals between each star shaped bead

11. Extension chain: String one end of the chain onto the other jump ring and close the jump ring. String the 4 mm crystal bead onto the 2.5 cm head pin and trim the head pin to ⅜" (1 cm). Make a loop in the head pin, draw it through the last link in the chain and close the loop.

To make even spaces along all three strands in this necklace, cut a 1" (2.5 cm) piece of cardboard and use it to measure the intervals between each star cluster.

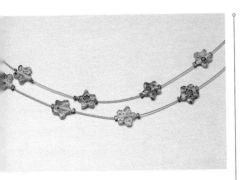

Arrange the beaded wires so that the stars don't overlap

Connect all three beaded wires with a cord tip

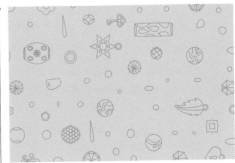

Shimmering Chandelier Earrings

Large yet delicate, these earrings maximize
the beauty of drop-shaped crystals by positioning
them at the bottom of large wire drops.

FINISHED MEASUREMENT	TOOLS	SKILL LEVEL
3½" (9 cm)	*Wire cutters* *Flat-nose pliers* *Round-nose pliers*	

MATERIALS

14" (36 cm) nylon-coated, stainless steel beading wire, 0.022" (0.55 mm)
6 green teardrop crystal beads, 8 mm
24 transparent white seed beads, 6°
24 gold-plated crimp beads, 1.5 mm
3 green teardrop crystal beads, 5 mm
18 transparent gold seed beads, 4°
12 brown oval crystal beads, 5 mm
2 gold-plated cord tips
1 pair gold-plated ear wires

(continued on page 118)

(continued from page 116)

1. Cut a 2½"(6.3 cm) piece of beading wire. String on a green teardrop crystal bead and draw it to the middle of the wire.

2. String 1 seed bead and 1 crimp bead on one side of the crystal. Make sure the crystal remains in the middle of the wire; then flatten the crimp bead.

3. Repeat step 2 on the other side of the teardrop crystal bead.

4. String 1 crimp bead onto the wire and draw it along until it is ⅜" (1 cm) from the flattened crimp bead. Flatten the crimp bead.

5. String 1 seed bead, 1 brown crystal bead, 1 seed bead and 1 crimp bead onto this end of the wire. Flatten the crimp bead.

6. Repeat steps 4 and 5 on the other side of the teardrop crystal.

7. Cut a 3½"(8.5 cm) piece of beading wire. String on a green teardrop crystal bead and draw it to the middle of the wire.

8. Repeat steps 2 and 3.

9. String a crimp bead onto the wire and draw it along until it is ½" (1.3 cm) from the flattened crimp

bead. Flatten the crimp bead and then repeat step 5.

10. Repeat step 9 on the other side of the teardrop crystal bead.

11. Cut a 5¼" (13 cm) piece of beading wire. String on a green teardrop crystal bead and draw it to the middle of the wire.

12. Repeat steps 2 and 3.

13. String a crimp bead onto the wire and draw it along until it is ⅗" (1.5 cm) from the flattened crimp bead. Flatten the crimp bead and then repeat step 5.

Materials

Sandwich each green crystal with seed beads and crimp beads

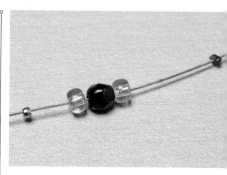

Sandwich each brown crystal with seed beads and crimp beads

14. Repeat step 13 on the other side of the teardrop crystal.

15. Gather together at both ends of all three wires and tuck them into a cord tip. Flatten the cord tip.

16. Open the loop at the bottom of 1 ear wire, string it through the loop in the cord tip and close the loop. Repeat steps 1 to 15 to make the matching earring.

•

Make sure the bead clusters are evenly spaced on both side of each strand in these earrings.

•

Leave even spaces between the bead clusters

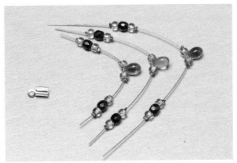

Connect all three wires with a cord tip

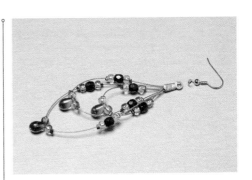

String the cord tip onto an ear wire

Gorgeously Green Gypsy Earrings

In these luminous earrings, the first and fifth strands are the same, as are the second and fourth strands. The third strand is a perfect place for showing off a really special pair of beads.

FINISHED MEASUREMENT

3½" (9 cm)

TOOLS

Wire cutters
Flat-nose pliers
Round-nose pliers

SKILL LEVEL

MATERIALS
20 emerald green oval crystal beads, 5 mm
10 pale yellow oval crystal beads, 5 mm
32 antique gold eye pins, 2.5 cm
4 antique gold bead caps
4 antique gold-plated leaf charms, 15 mm
2 antique gold-plated 5-loop drops
4 green flat-back round crystals, 3.9 mm
2 brown flat-back round crystals, 3.9 mm
Multipurpose glue
1 pair antique gold-plated 1-loop ear posts

(continued on page 122)

(continued from page 120)

1. Arrange beads in 5 columns, as follows:

Columns 1 and 5:

1 dark green crystal bead

1 pale yellow crystal bead

1 dark green crystal bead

Columns 2 and 4:

1 dark green crystal bead

1 pale yellow crystal bead

1 dark green crystal bead

1 leaf charm

Column 3:

1 dark green crystal bead

1 bead cap

1 pale yellow crystal

1 bead cap

1 dark green crystal bead

1 pale yellow crystal bead

2. String each bead in Column 1 onto an eye pin. Trim each eye pin to ⅜" (1 cm) and make a loop. Connect the eye pins in a chain and close the loops.

3. Repeat step 2 to string the beads for columns 2, 3, 4 and 5. Attach each column of beads to the appropriate loop in one gold-plated drop.

4. Apply a drop of glue to the back of three flat-back crystal and affix 3 crystals to the drop.

5. Open a jump ring. String it through the loop in 1 ear post and through the top loop in the drop. Close the jump ring.

6. Repeat steps 1 to 5 to make the matching earring.

Materials

Make a loop in each eye pin to connect the crystals

Connect one green, one yellow, and one green crystal

When choosing the components for these earrings, select ones that aren't too heavy. This is particularly important when selecting the earring drops.

Sandwich a yellow crystal between two bead caps

Attach the crystal chains to the gold-plated drops

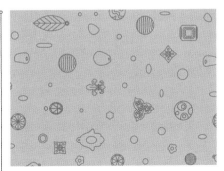

Charmed Chiming Ring

This ring will chime charmingly when you move your hand.
Impossible to miss, it's best worn alone, as it tends to upstage
other rings and accessories.

FINISHED MEASUREMENT

TOOLS

SKILL LEVEL

About 2" (5 cm)

Scissors
Round-nose pliers
Flat-nose pliers
Wire cutters

MATERIALS
Black leather fabric, 2 x ¾" (5 x 1 cm)
2 silver-plated textured cord tips, 1 cm
1 silver-plated jump ring, 6 mm
4 beads, various colors and styles, 5 to 10 mm
6 silver-plated bead caps
4 silver-plated head pins, 2 cm
1 large gold leaf, 1.5 cm
1 silver-plated split ring, 6 mm
1 silver-plated jump ring, 3 mm

(continued on page 126)

(continued from page 124)

1. Wrap the leather around your finger and trim it to size.

2. Insert each end of the leather into a cord tip; then flatten the cord tips.

3. Open the 6 mm jump ring and string it through the loop on each cord tip. Close the jump ring to connect the cord tips.

4. String the bead caps and beads onto the head pins as desired. Trim each head pin to ⅜" (1 cm) and make a closed loop.

5. String the decorated head pins onto the split ring. Open the 3 mm jump ring and use it to connect the split ring to the jump ring on the ring.

Materials

Insert each end of the leather into a cord tip

For a daintier ring, select leather that is narrower than 1 cm (and select suitable cord tips as well).

Connect the cord tips with a jump ring

Attach the beads to the leather ring using a jump ring

Crystal Bouquet Earrings

These dangling earrings are a sparkling twist on a common theme.
If you can't find open flower beads, try using a decorative bead cap instead.

FINISHED MEASUREMENT

2½" (6.3 cm)

TOOLS

Wire cutters
Round-nose pliers
Flat-nose pliers

SKILL LEVEL

MATERIALS

6 red faceted crystal beads, 5 mm
6 silver-plated open flower beads, 1 cm
6 silver-plated head pins, 2.5 cm
2 transparent white faceted round crystal beads, 12 mm
2 transparent white faceted round crystal beads, 8 mm
2 silver-plated eye pins, 3 cm
1 pair silver-plated ear wires

(continued on page 130)

(continued from page 128)

1. String 1 red crystal bead and 1 open flower bead onto a head pin. Trim the head pin to ⅜" (1 cm) and make a closed loop. Repeat once.

2. String a 12 mm white crystal onto an eye pin. String on the decorated head pins from step 1; then string on an 8 mm white crystal. Trim the head pin to ⅜" (1 cm) and make a loop. Don't close the loop.

3. String 1 red crystal bead and 1 open flower bead onto a head pin. Trim the head pin to ⅜" (1 cm) and make a loop. Don't close the loop.

4. String the decorated head pin from step 3 onto the bottom loop of the eye pin and close the loop.

5. String the top loop in the decorated eye pin through the loop at the bottom of the ear wire. Close the loop.

6. Repeat steps 2 to 5 to make the matching earring.

Materials

String a red crystal and an open flower bead onto a head pin

This design creates the impression of a sparkling red rose garden. Create a multicolored garden by replacing some of the red crystals with vibrant pink or yellow ones.

String white crystals and decorated head pins onto the eye pin

String a decorated head pin onto the bottom of the eye pin

Connect the earring to an ear wire

Hanging Garden Earrings

These easy-to-make earrings dangle delightfully on a bare neck.
Wear them with upswept hair for maximum effect.

FINISHED MEASUREMENT **TOOLS** **SKILL LEVEL**

2¾" (7 cm)

Wire cutters
Flat-nose pliers
Round-nose pliers

MATERIALS
5" (13 cm) rose-gold, small-link chain
2 flat rose-gold, 4-hole flower beads, 10 mm
2 rose-gold cord tips, 1 mm
2 gold-plated head pins, 3 cm
2 round white pearls, 15 mm
2 round gold pearls, 12 mm
1 pair rose-gold ear wires

(continued on page 134)

(continued from page 132)

1. Cut the chain into two 2½" (6.3 cm) pieces.

2. Fold 1 piece of chain in half. Insert each end of the chain through one of the holes at the bottom of 1 flower bead, and draw the chain ends up through the top holes. Pull the chain upwards until a U-shaped piece of chain hangs below the flower.

3. Insert both ends of the chain into a cord tip and flatten the cord tip.

4. String a white pearl and a gold pearl onto a head pin. Trim the head pin to ⅜" (1 cm) and make a loop. Don't close the loop.

5. String the loop in the head pin onto the middle link in the chain below the flower bead. Close the loop.

6. Open the loop at the bottom of 1 ear wire and string it onto the loop at the top of the cord tip. Close the loop.

7. Repeat steps 2 to 6 to make the matching earring.

Materials

Connect both ends of the chain with a cord tip

If you want a more dramatic look, add another bead or two to the pearls that are strung on the dangling head pin.

String a white pearl and a gold pearl onto a head pin

Connect the earring to an ear wire

Crystal Hoop Earrings

In just a few minutes, this dangling design dresses up
a simple pair of hoop earrings. For a completely different look,
change the color or type of beads.

FINISHED MEASUREMENT	TOOLS	SKILL LEVEL
2½" (6.5 cm)	*Wire cutters* *Round-nose pliers*	

MATERIALS

8 dark brown round faceted crystal beads, 4 mm
6 pink round faceted crystal beads, 4 mm
6 light brown round faceted crystal beads, 4 mm
1 pair gold-plated hoop earrings, 5 cm
6 gold-plated head pins, 2 cm

(continued on page 138)

(continued from page 136)

1. String 1 dark brown crystal bead onto a hoop earring.

2. String a light pink crystal bead and a light brown crystal bead onto a head pin. Trim the head pin to ⅜" (1 cm) and make a closed loop. String the loop onto the hoop earring.

3. String 1 light brown crystal bead onto a hoop earring.

4. String a dark brown crystal bead and a pink crystal bead onto a head pin. Trim the head pin to ⅜" (1 cm) and make a closed loop. String the loop onto the hoop earring.

5. String 1 pink crystal bead onto a hoop earring.

6. String a light brown crystal bead and a dark brown crystal bead onto a head pin. Trim the head pin to ⅜" (1 cm) and make a closed loop. String the loop onto the hoop earring.

7. String 1 dark brown crystal bead onto a hoop earring.

8. Repeat steps 1 to 7 to make the matching earring.

Materials

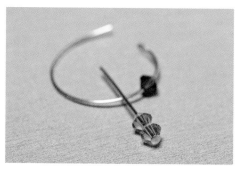

String a crystal and a decorated head pin onto a hoop earring

Don't worry if the loops on each head pin aren't identical since each dangling head pin is sandwiched by crystal beads. That makes this design particularly good for beginners.

String another crystal and decorated head pin onto the hoop earring

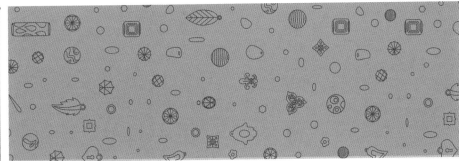

Luscious Cherry Earrings

These vibrant, clustered earrings are
both lush and luxurious. For a matching bracelet, see the
Royal Harvest Bracelet (pages 24 to 27).

FINISHED MEASUREMENT	TOOLS	SKILL LEVEL
3" (7.5 cm)	Wire cutters Round-nose pliers	

MATERIALS

5" (13 cm) gold-plated, small-link chain
36 red and gold round beads, 5 to 6 mm
36 gold-plated head pins, 2 cm
1 pair gold-plated ear wires

(continued on page 142)

(continued from page 140)

1. Cut the chain into two 2½" (6.3 cm) pieces. Divide the beads into two groups, so that each group has a similar collection of beads. Arrange the beads in each group in a line. Try to make the order of beads similar in both groups.

2. String each bead onto a head pin. Trim the head pins to ⅜" (1 cm) and make a loop. Don't close the loop.

3. String the bottommost bead in one of the groups onto the bottom link of one piece of chain. Close the loop.

4. String the next bead onto the link immediately above the bottom link.

Close the loop in the head pin. String the next bead on the other side of the same link and close the loop.

5. Repeat step 4 until all the beads in one group have been strung onto one of the chains. If there are empty links at the top of the chain, you may remove them.

6. Open the loop at the bottom of 1 ear wire and string it through the link at the top of the chain. Close the loop.

7. Repeat steps 3 to 6 to make the matching earring.

Materials

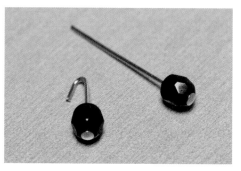

String each bead onto a head pin
and make a loop

Make sure the links in your chain aren't too small so that you can comfortably string on the head pins.

Connect each head pin to a chain link

Attach an ear wire to the top chain link

Index